Blessing of the Sun

Christine Berger

Letters

Concrescent Letters

For information contact:
Concrescent Letters, an imprint of Concrescent LLC
Richmond CA, USA
info@Concrescent.net

ISBN: 978-0-9843729-6-6

Library of Congress Control Number: 2012941791

Contents

Emancipation Song
09-02-11

Recently given virulent feedback from
my one still living parent
a week of being sick while I contemplated severing ties
conspired together to bring me to a breakthrough
Tonight driving home, my time
for contemplation

Here is my history as I reconstructed it:

Momma did not get the baby girl she wanted
She wanted curls and softness and pliant behavior
She got a scrawny tomboy with ideas of her own
and everything possible was done to bring the girl into line
with that which was taught and valued and acceptable
in the fifties, after all, what would the neighbors think?

Momma did not like the teenage strangeness
the disobedient, boy crazy bundle of adventurous
hormones
So she did all she could to convey that sexuality was evil
unless it was firmly leashed by marriage and then we
just did not talk
about it
bleeding was bad and so was the female body
All that was wild and pulsing and explosive contrary to propriety
Was to be bound, constrained and brought into line
The plan was already drawn up, had been since birth

Daddy loved his little girl but was confused by her willfulness
Everything was established, all was provided for
work hard in school, ignore the boys
Listen to Momma
go get a degree, play the piano
be a good reflection of the middle class values
and then, but only then, Momma and Daddy will love you
just the way you are.

Not until many years later
when Daddy was gone and Momma left alone
and Daughter still trying to set adult boundaries to
protect her essence
and honor a relationship of mutual respect
was it noted by Momma that everything that was real to Daughter
was considered an insult and a deliberate affront
just to shock the dear old lady.

This is my song:

The ties that have bound me from childhood
Are sundered as the chains are shattered
I see who I am and who I want to be
and all the deliberate attempts to kill that off are now vanquished

My sex is alive
Vibrant
Healthy
Celebratory
Loving
Giving
Meant to be shared and delighted in. a Gift!
the vital life force that makes me smile and dance and laugh
that makes my bare feet stomp on Momma Earth and her vibrations
rise up and carry me further into our dance

My mind is coming more alive each day
The joy I had in learning before I was forced into
memorizing only that which bored me
and gave up,
is my birthright
is who I am
is my very Spirit seeking to be more, to experience more
To communicate more, and to create
to touch and breathe and partake of Reality
with every breath that I take

My body embraces Life with every cell
Such Joy
To be brought through a passage with unknown causes
and unknown endings, to finally arrive at endgame
and left more open and more sensitive
with nerve endings antennas for the electric song of the Universe
there are plants and trees and skies and suns and moons and stars
Rivers and oceans and animals of all sizes and shapes
humans and half divines and divine beings, beings I cannot
even define
Mysteries in living rocks that shine and talk and heal
Telling secrets I am just beginning to learn to hear

This is my world
My purpose plays hide go seek with me
my desire to be healer and lover and sister and mother
Elder and wise woman and oh so very young in a Universe
as vast and mighty
as this one
I will not be bound by anyone's expectations, not even
my own
nor will I believe the lies they planted within me so many
years ago
I and my Maker together create this life anew each day.

And it is Good. And it is Dark. And it is Light. And it is
Never Ever Boring.

A' Walkin'
03-29-11

I will go a walkin'
down the fog drenched paths
on the moors
amongst the heather and bracken
the smell of the sea in my skin
Drawing solace from my solitude
and the feel of the Mother beneath my feet

I will go a walkin'
through dappled afternoons
Deep into the forest whose scent
brings me deep into myself
and all it means to be Daughter of the Earth
to know the richness of the soil
that brings forth life from death
constantly taking the cycle around and bout

I will go a walkin'
in desert sands in a land
that knows that life comes with the water
all that grows arises from the nourishment
that great Lady brings to the land
If She is generous all live
If She withholds her favor
None can focus upon anything but her Grace
and the need for the river to flow once again

I will go a walkin'
on the village shore, both loving and fearing this deep water
Sheltered in her coves and embraced by her warmth
or waiting there for the harvest the men bring to us
and praying that this day She does not harvest from us
Their strength but brings them home to safe harbor
once again

My grandmothers sing me this song
they flow in the rhythm of my hips
They show me the faces and forms I have worn
All the colors and shapes
and underneath it all their strength and beauty
Lives again in me each time
I know of their sacrifices and their joys
I know of men who brought up children
Without a mother while the land itself held them
This plumb line goes deep, I see neither its beginning
Nor its end.

Christine Berger

Calling on the Ancestors

10-19-10

Riding the grace wave
Grateful for the break
Is it because I am getting further away
From the injection point?
Just the gift of the Universe?
A result of talking to my
Great Grandmother Beck?
All of the above?

Makes no difference
I will make the most of the
Interval
Where I feel like myself
Body spirit and mind

My Great Grandmother Beck
Was fully lucid and brilliant
Well into her eighties
When I met her as a little girl

To this day I remember the impression she made
Upon me
Today I called upon her
Asking for a strengthening
Of the mental clarity that I felt slipping and sliding yesterday
I hedge my bets
I call on all my allies
Been talking to Hermes a lot
Guess who has been in the driver's seat
On the freeways in the am
And at seven o'clock at night coming home
After ten hour days

In my right mind
I know
As my Dad used to say
What side my bread is buttered on..

What does it mean to be a magician?
A witch?
A light worker?
A healer?

To me it feels like being a surfer
Knowing which wave to catch at the perfect moment
Feels like being a bird in flight
Adjusting the angle of my wings
Depending on the predominant currents

Driving in this morning
At the point where I send Reiki
To all my relations
I reached out with all my Being
Feeling seeing tasting their presence
In joy and union

In that moment
I saw the birds flock overhead
Heard the gulls cry
Witnessed a moment of the perfection
Of the Natural world

I have been meditating again
I reach for every tool every life line
Every feathered wing
Every surfboard
Every sweet current
Every taste of My Lover's lips

However that may manifest

Christine Berger

Coming to smell the honeysuckle
08-25-09

Choosing to take longer than the rules bade me
I walked to the honeysuckle bush
Thrusting my nose into the freshest flower
I breathed deep as the scent filled me
As always that scent is summer
Is warm sensual nights
Is soft heat that entices
My cells and that scent intertwined

Calling the wild God in the morning
On the drive in
I felt him come
His energy strong primal and very much
Of the body
As I walked back
I caught his scent in swift glances
To the pine
The grasses
The shadows space between patches of sunlight

The sky perfect crystalline blue
Beckoned to me
Calling " release release the weight you need not carry "
The juice of the blackberries warmed in the sun
Tart and sweet
Thrilling in potency to awake
That essence of me which is only happy
With bare toes on earth
Sun and wind or starry cloaked night
In my face
Over my head
Calling me to memories of perfect bliss

I am Child of Earth
Child of Spirit
Child of Sky and Star
Child of Ocean
All these have made me
And they make me still

I do not belong in these concrete buildings
My song is not sung in steel and paper and ledger sheets
My song is howled at the moon
My song rises in ecstasy
As my lover comes with me
My song dances in Life itself
It will not be obscured by all
That these men do
To keep themselves busy and removed
From that which keeps them breathing

My lover was the breeze that softly caressed my neck
before I went back in.

Beauty in the commonplace
05-03-09

There is that hunger within me
Always looking for intensity
For the extraordinary
For the mystery to be revealed
Yet what is present in everyday life
Is not to be undervalued

If properly aligned
Whatever life brings me
To do
To reflect upon
To understand
To accept
Is extraordinary

Can I forget that being in form
Itself
Is a gift?
Breathe in
Breathe out
Heart pumping
All systems go in vitality and health
Oh, Love, this is a miracle
You awake to every day

To see your heart's light
Reflected in the face of
Lover or friend
To look into the face of
Cat or child
To feel the ethereal embrace
Of life on the planet
In kingdoms
Of plant
Animal
Mineral
All these have depth and dimension
Beyond first glance

The Universe is never inconsequential
Whether it be a singular atom
Or a super nova or star system
Break through the facade of human perception
And like that first acid trip
Vision leads to expansion
Surpassing all comprehension

Being alone suffices.

Blown open
10-21-10

Embracing the core
The current rises from Earth to center
From Sky to center
From center to the web
Within and without
The difference is a magic show
That we mistake for reality

This moment struck me after a lovely walk
With the storm riding in
Everything was more alive
Charged
Vibrating on the edge of massive change
It was exhilarating

I had a moment of realization
That were any one of us to come face to face
With what we really are
Without the ground work to prepare us
We would go mad with the breadth
The depth
The intensity of the experience

Then I remembered a strange period of my life
Not long before I met the lodge
I had a house guest
A Cherokee elder
Who had come to prepare for a wedding
of friends
There was so much light and unwinding going on
During his visit
He warned me at a certain point
That I should slow down on what I was receiving

Ignoring the warning
The repercussion was for several days
I was literally blown open
Non-functional

A lesson was learned that day
I do not ask to learn as fast as possible any more
I ask to learn
To have the courage to navigate my lessons
Fearlessly and with heart

Shortly after that time, my entire outer support system
Completely collapsed
I was isolated for the next year
Working to rebuild
Then met the lodge at Pantheacon

There are reasons we meditate
Do exercises to open mind body and spirit
On a daily basis
Establish a structure
That is capable of holding the current

When the time is right to let it rip
Well prepared
We will fly and expand and unite
Not be blown away

Blessing of the Sun
02-15-10

Sitting with Sun Love
Pouring over my shoulders
Into my head
My neck
My heart
Willing the letting go
To the sweet heat
Sweet healing energy
Reminding me that
I am perfectly loved
Each and every moment
It is not that there were not incidents
Moments of stress
Witness to at least one psychotic break
In the environment
I knew how to give and get the necessary healing
Revive my spirits on all levels
With my favorite faery tribe
More than once
So the gifts of grace
Far surpassed any of the dark shadows
Oh Momma, the gifts
Meeting Daddy Down Under
At the crossroads within
Tears pouring down my face
Remembering the power
Of His integration in my world
I asked for the necessary help
The power of dancing in the center
At the Red God Revel
The heat built until the point of release
Sweat pouring down my body
I was Fire translated to Water
Cleansed on all levels
The gift that surpassed all for me
Was being allowed to be a part of
A channel for another's healing
While roses bloomed and united

For a precious indescribable moment
We were one being consciously immersed
In transformation
Love strengthened
Love revealed
Love deepened
Oh my tribe!
Never in this lifetime
Have I had better mirrors of the best
bits of Spirit in form
The joy of the dance of the Lady
In all her facets
With the Lord in all of his
Bypassing and tweaking and laughing at
Gender identifications
Reveling
Revealing
This eternal dance that creates the Universe
Moment by moment in this thing we experience
as Time...
Within me
Without me
Letting Love
Desire
Laughter
Joy
Music
Dance
Ritual
Healing
Compersion
Unity experience beyond all
Thought possible
Play out again
All that is left to say is
Thank You.

Sex and Nature
01-18-10

Found my break coincided nicely
To a dry spell near work today
Yet the winds were fierce and cold and powerful
I found the stormy atmosphere intrinsically
Sexy
Invigorating
Foreplay
Primal Male Essence
Primal Female Essence

Riding home in the car
It seemed to me that Nature is always in
An orgasmic state
If we were open
Fearless
Beings
We were created to be
We would be sharing that state 24/7

Think of oceans leaving their foam upon the earth
Sunshine sparkling on the waters
Waves flicking their spume to the ever present air
Hot tropical jungles
Rainforests
Breathing in and out with the life force of the planet
As do we

Think of primal forests
Plants in all their glory springing from their seeds
In the ground
Making sunshine into their bodies
Feeding all life here with light

Think of star-shine and moonshine
Penetrating the deep soulful darkness
Of the everlasting night sky
Think of luminosity in perfect stillness

Think of the night giving birth each dawn
To the unblemished possibility of the new day

How is it living between heaven and earth
That we do not celebrate Life every moment

I dance as I witness the joy my body experiences as it
moves

Transmission and Reception
09-30-10

Standing over the canal
On this bit of land I love
Like a child loves its Mother
This prayer came to me

Earth and water below me
Fire and air above me
I call upon you my friends
Awaken the wisdom centers within me
That I may find my way

Earth Mother below me
Horned God before me
I call upon you my friends
Awaken the wisdom centers within me
That I may know my path

Opening my eyes all was perfect
All was Beauty
I closed my eyes again
The wind was fierce and cool and wonderful
As it blew away my troubles and my sorrows
I asked to be made bigger
To be taken out of the self obsession that can come
with challenge
While still embracing the delicate balance and tiny being I am
So perfectly held in the arms
Of the Universe which made me

Walking back I was transformed
At peace
A quiet joy
I know that I must navigate this maze
Under my own sails
Have too much fear or crumble or battle with authority figures
And I lose my way
The answers for this body, this life are within me
Once I find that certainty
Then I must hold fast
Without anger or antagonism

My doctor is not my enemy
But my job is to tend this precious vehicle
That enables me to be here
To love and to learn
To have something to give

If part of my wyrd is to be a bridge
In my life experience
Between East and West
Alternative and allopathic
Then I must simultaneously be open to new information
While fiercely holding to the center of that which I know
Nurtures my well being.

Blaze of Glory
09-09-10

I am not finished
I ain't dead yet
I struggled for survival the first month of my life
Yet I am here sixty years and change later
I am not a weak sister
I am not a coward
I have been given much and I will give back
Until the last breath in this body

Seeds planted in the fertile ground of the nineteen year old
In 1968
Have borne fruit
this life is precious to me
I have found new love which makes me smile in wonder every day
My world blooms with love of every scent
that I have desired
I want to teach
To spread Reiki as far and as wide as possible
To watch it come alive in blending with new modalities
New Masters
There are universes for me to learn about
and learn to play about

This virus is proving to be one of the very best teachers
Though I have tasted my darkness and walked the edge
of the cliff
Of self annihilation
More than once
It is in facing this challenge
that I am becoming most alive
If my days might be shorter than my desire
then I must burn brighter
Learn faster
Give of myself more
Listen better
and reach farther
While letting go of any preconceived result

My liver informs me I spend too much time
with useless anger and stress
Over circumstances that are just the play of consciousness
in its dying and its rebirth in this time on this earth
The Big Picture is neither my business nor my job
It is for me to witness while I do the full time work
of minding my own business
One price of free will is that I am surrounded by
aspects of the one that may not be doing things
Exactly the way I want them to
If I have time to focus on that with that attitude
You can bet your ass that my own house is dirty

I am full of life
My sexuality rising like a Phoenix from the ashes
As it dances with Love and Delight and Spirit
I am changed daily
I seek the stillness within
as my strength lies there
But I will not stand still
Moaning that the winds of change are crippling me
If they can knock my legs out from under me
I better build up more strength

To say I am missing necessary ingredients
to complete the task
Whether I have a day
Or decades left
Is to cop out
to give lie to all that has been invested
the Universe in the last week has been showering me with
Encouragement
Healings
Love
Gifts of every kind of tool
From the image on my Eastern bedroom wall
Of the God I love
to the crystals here and on their way

I will no longer cower nor tremble nor hide
I am here
I will do what I was put here to do
I am a creature of happiness and joy
that is my birthright and my responsibility
to release each day

I remembered to sing this chant yesterday
On my walk in Corte Madera
Which I believe Thorn taught many years ago in a class
at Pantheacon

" Let it begin with every step I take"
" Let it begin with every change I make"
" Let it begin with every chain I break"
" Let it begin with every day I wake"

I shall live my life to the fullest until I cannot
I request that the God who guards my daily journeys
Guides my final one home when it is time.
Meanwhile, there is work I love still to do.

Butterflies in the Temple
03-18-10

Strange days indeed
The Mother sustains me
In the ley lined sacred ground near work
I make it through my days because of this
Though exhaustion claims me once the sun
Goes down

But it is the joy of my walks that
rises up and fills me and marks my days
When I was young in the sixties
During the period where LSD
Was the drug of choice
Some nights I was not even stoned
But my teacher and guide was
Her contemplation of the Universe
in Discourse carried me through those long
Holy nights

My favorite time before
Succumbing to sleep
Was Dawn
there is something inherently and deeply sacred to me
About bird songs when the sun rises

There is that quality when I do my ten am walk
The light is still the ephemeral delicate morning light
The birds, especially as the wakefulness of Spring approaches,
Have that sweet unique song greeting the light, the trees, the world
As they experience it
They set the first tone, these small winged messengers of love
My heart opens

Once I start to open on the walk
The sun starts to penetrate that cakra
I can feel it enter
I remind myself to keep walking
to keep chanting for the earth
As that is usually what I do

the crows watch me now
Knowing that I leave offerings for Hermes
They prepare to snatch them as quickly as possible
Not afraid of me at all
They are at their best, bold and proud

I am so deeply in love with this area
This small bit of Corte Madera
has captured me
It is perfection
It is power, Natural power
It is a portal for Love
For the Earth Herself
For the Gods and Goddesses I may be called
To contemplate

There is a park in the wealthy section
Perfectly circular
Thick plush grass
With towering trees
one small area of steps of concrete covered by moss
Concrete benches arranged in the circle
Also covered by moss
At one time men shaped it
But it belongs to the other world now

This afternoon I approached it
Fully aware of the power alive in it
The God's presence was there
Healing was given

I have not been in this area this time of year
I was bombarded by butterflies today
Those who live in the area take it for granted
They are tiny golden black and orange butterflies
colored somewhat like Monarchs
but very tiny
They flutter across the road in groups of five or six or seven
they nearly fly into your face

each time they startled me
Laughter rose from my child's heart
Looking at my shadow on the sidewalk as I strode
With purpose and feminine delight
I knew the ageless part of me
and rejoiced

Brillantes Estrellas
04-22-10

Today my Mama told me
Use the healing power of music
Take your walk as I have given you sunshine
Let the healing flow
Let go of all the pain and sorrow

I moved to the music
These words came to me
It is my obligation to Dance
It is my obligation to emit Joy
It is my obligation to take
The sunshine, the blue sky air
The plant kingdom majesty
These things that feed me
And send it back forth to all
In joy in dance in song in healing

Coming back Thorn and Sharon's
Beautiful song came on
Everything shifted to the Holy Place
Where only She exists
The hand gesture sprung up naturally
Palm up to receive
Palm down to feed Gaia
I did it all the way through the song

I did not stop when the stroller
Came towards me
The nanny would not care
The indigo child made eye contact
His smile a secret message
Heart to Heart
He looked at my hand gestures
Then smiled wider as our eyes connected our souls

Thank you, Mama.

We are brilliant stars

All of us
Rather than lose our way in the maelstrom
Let us shine more fiercely more boldly more fearlessly
It is our obligation.

All I Really Want
09-15-10

It's all about the love
This energy has been running through me
The last twenty four hours
I suspect other than the known healing done for me last night
Much is happening behind the scenes
All I know is that I am in love
With everything

Walking down the busy Oakland streets
Near the hospital today there were gardens
Roses as high as me in all different colors
The light in the sky through the fog
The folks sitting next to me in line
Everything carried radiance
Though I could not see it
I could feel it

I am a cup
A vessel
Shaped of moonlight and silver
Sweet wine of love poured into me
Overflows and must be sent forth

Radiating from me in Golden Light
Through Reiki
Through just the burning desire I carry
To send it forth
As Love must be shared to stay alive

I am a child still held tenderly
Still safe
In fact this child feels more secure
Than I did in my physical childhood
Much obstruction has been removed
I have been altered
Changed for the better
Softer and more open
Resilient from a faith born through experience

I was told today
If I get scared or
Worry about the future
To say to myself or out loud
"There is only Now"

And now is only Love

Sweet End of the Morning Commute
07-14-11

After I get through the Oakland end
madness of 580 and the maze
and then the approach to the San Rafael bridge
which in itself can be challenging as well
the sweet part is getting off the exit for Sr Francis Drake
headed into Larkspur and Corte Madera

At this point having done my morning Reiki and prayers
while I roll down the windows and breathe the beauty
of the morning
into me
While I contemplate the inputs of the morning

This morning that ranged from Stone Kettle and the madness
of politics as it is currently to my yoga practice
and the Dakini Oracle of Nurtura as well as morning
runes and tarot card

suddenly I switched radio stations and caught
the last half of This Sex is on Fire
In fierce contrast to the contractions instigated by
those instruments of change
Who are visibly in power on the stage now
Suddenly the vision of the enormous Heat and Love
That truly is Universe arose
I could feel the immensity of that energy
and my Desire was that all living beings were so fired up
With that Love that Desire for union with Life embodied
in God Herself
That the visible world be transformed for all of our sakes

And I was allowed for the moment a taste
of that Reality.

Walking in the Sunshine Wearing Amber
08-12-10

I am in love with these walks
A mess when I went out from stress in the cube
The first thing I realized was that my favorite amber necklace
Which I think of as a bird's nest
Was happily having conversation with the sun
Since I was wearing it my heart center was getting some lovely juice
As well

This place
This earth
This Sun
These trees and birds and deer
All of these heal me
In this place I feel like I belong
Like I am an organic part of the landscape
Though the reality is the same wherever I walk
The feeling with intensity behind it occurs here.

Looking at the canal that serves the bay tides
I saw little tiny fish
Which I realized are what the egrets are most likely
Stalking
Thinking of them as egret food
Made me laugh
What am I food for?
The day will come when this body
Will feed something

My thoughts were happy and remembering
All the things that bring deep joy
I remembered my lover's kiss
At out last greeting
In my imagination
The satisfaction of that moment
Was that of a cat
Licking up a dollop of heavy cream
Off her whiskers
Happiness rides sunshine and amber and sex

Learning to Sculpt
07-29-11

As a youth I was full of wonder, innocence
unflagging sexuality
and untested optimism
I miss my sunny disposition
but it was born in the naivety of a child

After a most intense week
and some conclusive changes today
I began to comprehend a bit of my long stay
In the sphere of water
It is not just that I am comfortable here
But it is that learning emotional control
does not come easy
It is as if I am sculpting my own nature
in order to gain it
with the pain of carving a living being
me
into new shapes

my 32 weeks subjected to Western medicine were to
carve away fear
and to recognize that if mind and body
were stripped down
to basics
Spirit was waiting to carry me securely protected
This was the exorcising of fear
Culminating in taking the step to go against
Medical advice and listen to the internal
and physical demand to cease and desist

For three days the week began
without sleep for 36 hours and then
I was caught in a net of mourning and grief and
Loss
Tied to issues of abandonment
and not belonging that came with me
through that first month of life in isolation
No wonder I have issues with hospitals

They made poor parents those early days
It was a rough passage
sometimes the shaping goes quickly
sometimes it is particle by particle
Each time though there is a lightness of being
A confirmation that the work has been worth it

The most stubborn of the patterns
the most difficult to detach and step back from
Is a deep seated anger
under the stress at work and issues
of respect when my boss hits her stress limit
Left me on the edge the last two days
Sitting at the reception desk for a short break
I invoked Freya, whose shirt I was wearing
Three times I took all that bottled up energy
And powered my call

And was answered

three times asked
To remove this anger that rages out of all proportion
to the triggers in the environment
Unnecessary, and unproductive
It is not the impersonal anger arising that demands that
we protect
those who are trammeled or abused before us

Again I was answered

It seems to me that if I can direct some of that
frustrated
Martial energy bound by conjunction with Saturn
and direct it towards accomplishing my will
It will be a wonderful ally
Much better than me using it to throw stones
at these targets I erect.

As so often happens on the ley lines
The shifts are very evident in the energy
The results of change in thought or feeling are
Instantly powered by the Earth Herself
both missteps and course correction crystal clear
Because everything is amplified.

When I have made enough progress here
I can proceed with the mercurial portion demanded so I
can play in fire
my natal home plate
I know there is a great fountain of burning optimism
As bright as the sun
waiting for me there.

Blazing Within
07-08-11

Just as the flame burns for one Lover
So does it burn for all that is
For kith and kin
For Universe
For all who guide my steps and open my heart
For Life itself

A visual has been trying to arise
The heart burning with a golden sun
Flame rising the sacred tunnel that houses the serpent force
Feet bare and sunk into sweet earthy mud as a child
would wiggle their toes
From the arms branches of a great tree embrace with
fertile growth
A cross beam
As sky and star energy of utter luminosity pours
through the crown
Even contemplating this achieves a state of bliss

Nothing has or can save my Life
Other than this Love that breathes through everything
I perceive
In the blaze of its glory
The lies of sad lost children chasing a power that does
not even exist
become smoke rings
insubstantial and blown away

This one gift of Love
is not separable into pieces or fragments
There is no difference between what I feel
whatever or whoever the focus
Though some trigger more intensity in my inner flamboyance
Than others
Some are softer and sooth
Some mix the passion born of steam
Fire and water in union.
and some go deep and still into the Earth Mother.,

Words Cannot Fly
02-20-10

In deep dark places that carry all worlds
words are frail not the sign posts
post cards are not the essence
Gifted only through that which inspires
that which sustains
that which holds all
they can be the arrow that pierces the illusions

They can carry the energy of the Love
though they will never equal the impact
of its arrow penetrating the center
Impaled on that point all is still
all is the sweetest energy rising
from the depths within

These days I am learning
of this Love affair which has captured me
heart and soul and being
She has captured me
Nay awakened me to the reality
That I was never less than Hers
In service in delight in surrender in passion
In willing action enabled by her current

this is what has carried me from day to night
from lifetime to lifetime
from the lost child
of my youth
following the quietest voice
To the dancing child of now
with ears only to hear the voice
That stills all else

I live to walk through the deep dark places
Through the woods
Through the caves
through the silences far from
That which was known
To that which is ever revealing

      I dance on the starlight carrying the secret code
carried in my blood and bone

Where She leads I will follow

Unravel Me
08-21-11

Working through the yoga and savasana
Praying that the knots in my hips and back
would be released
the imprints of driving, sitting and stressing
Too much
on top of an area that was off kilter upon entry
this time around

This prayer sprung to mind

Unravel me
Remove the knots in my body
That keep the energy from flowing freely
receiving and giving healing through this vehicle
which is a unique gift allowing me to be present
in this time and this place, to witness and wonder
to learn, to love, to dance the dance of life

Unravel me
Remove the bindings of the reptilian brain
whose sole focus is survival and domination
take me to the realms of my allies
Beloved dragon kin
Who embrace the Great Pearl of Wisdom
and bring blessings to all they encounter

Unravel me
let the bindings of my mind be loosened
from the ego driven bondage of sanskaras
patterns that are outmoded from this life
and others
Keeping me from the bright intelligence
which is always revealing more, teaching more
fresh and fast and illuminating
that tiny glimpse of God Herself
as she spins universes out
and draws them back within

    Unravel me
Let my Heart and the Love it serves
be free of patterns of duality
such as fear and abandonment and that loneliness
That comes from the lie of separation
Let Spirit and Love rejuvenate that which I call Self

Owning the Broken Bits
08-20-11

Last night was one of the more painful
as I found myself in the wee hours of the morning
Caught in the embrace of the cut off feeling within
That feeling of being completely empty and disconnected
from Love
I was but a husk, a hull, an empty shell
and the pain was incredible

It probably did not last as long as it seemed
I grabbed two crystals and started the Reiki
Not as a "cure" so much as to be able to endure the state
I was in
In order to Be in it without further contraction

It is easy when loving is the natural state
and somewhere I live more often than in the past
to not want to acknowledge and experience its antithesis
a coldness
A hard selfish kernel that is composed of fear
withholding and ego desire beyond all else

One of the greatest gifts of the last couple of years
and a result of the catalyzing influence of those I am closest to
is the slowly ingrained habit of truly looking at the bits
and pieces that come up to the surface
This broken selfish hardhearted
child was mine
was as much "me"
as the parts so easy to love and nurture

I wept for that part that is the source of all pain
Within and without
How dare I think that those qualities that repel me
in the collective mirrors of the world
were something other than mine as well.

as release came in accepting the pain and sharpness
of these sharp fragments
as if walking barefoot on glass
the realization came that I truly do not want to serve
or manifest anything other than Love

Circumstances, where I live, how I make my living
Even who I am privileged to count as friends and lovers
Are reflections of how freely that river flows
If I am alone,
or held in the warm embrace and presence of like minded companions
That lifeline is what fuels my being
It is what gets me up in the morning
Enables me to maneuver through my days
and release my cares in the sweet rocking of the night

If the riverbed has rocks that sometimes seem so big
as to damn up the flow
I have the time and the will to break it down
or to dive into the deep pool created
while I sort through and choose to let go of
or use the materials at hand to build to create to shape
a life more in accord with Love.

Venus conjunct the Sun
12-03-09

The walk started with awareness of blockage
Which is unusual when I walk the earth near work
As the area is a healing and magical place for me
So I do what I always do
I chanted and then I just started talking to Mom
Letting her know I needed some healing
In my heart center

I kept walking
Kept the chant going
When I saw an image of a damn on a river stream
Being busted up so that the flow could happen
At the same time I felt the blockages and damn
Restricting the flow of love within
Several releases happened
As if pieces of armoring were being pulled out of me
Simultaneously the crows started hollering
As I opened with gratitude and joy

I saw another vision of the snow in a mountain stream
Being melted by a powerful spring Sun
Its flow speeding up
I passed into the state where I am making love
To everything around me
The trees
The sky
The ducks
The crows
The earth holding me

I looked up in the sky
There were three pairs of crows
Spiraling and swooping and playing with each other
I had to laugh
It was marvelous

The feeling of opening continued
Much of the way home
Driving towards the mountains in Larkspur
To get gas
The mountain was mostly in shadow
But the top third of it was in perfect sunlight
Bathing in golden light
I was at a stoplight and had a chance to just observe
As I felt that golden light change the world
Saw the auras of the evergreens before me

Loving the natural magic that sustains and heals me
At the point where I am tired of struggling
With cleaning house

Temple of Love
08-29-11

In the wee hours of the night
when sleep was only a figment of the imagination
the Priestess burned from toes to head
I heard her sing this song

I am a Temple of Love
the candle wick for its flame to burn
from the wax at the root which rises from the earth
to the smoke offering itself to the heavens above
My purpose to serve
The Act of Love, the Art of Love, the Heart of Love

When I burn my midnight oil
There is no object of my affections
Unless it be God Herself
Once I have been set aflame
Only She can quench me
As this Flame is eternal
and never ceases its burning
nor my heart its yearning
to simply be Hers.

In the day I tend to my duties
Most of those around me cannot see
How I burn
As I clean and nourish and flow like water
in my surroundings, invisible to most
Serving Her will in my offerings
of self to Self
as there is no other

On occasion I will meet another
So afflicted by Fire and Water
We will smile tenderly
with our eyes our lips and hearts
For we know there can be a release in the intensity
For a moment in sharing the heat of the Fire
Spirit sends its cool Light
From above
as the moon can cool and calm the sun

When my bed is not empty
I do not burn alone
and that is where I receive Her peace.

Aye Aye Aye
01-31-10

Today was a first experience of this
In order to eliminate my headache
Get a proper start to my day
Knowing if I don't do yoga in the am
I will find a hundred distractions later
I proceeded with one of my favorite online Classes

All was resolved including the headache
No surprises whatsoever
Until I got to the corpse pose at the end
As always I align at the end with Dragon kin
Reiki Masters and Guides
Earth Mother and Horned God
A time of prayer and meditation

Except today in the midst of relaxing
The hunger rose again
It has no sense of timing
Or to be more accurate
It claims all time that I am embodied
As its own

The change today was that I now have
Fantasies of being with you
Here
In my home
Face to face
Body to body
Touching on all levels
It walks the edge of nervousness and excitement and joy

Something has shifted
With our last connection
The enhancement of the most powerful
Full moon I have felt in ages
I am inclined to the following conclusion

If I trust you

I trust you to be responsible for your life
On all levels

If I trust me
I trust myself to do the same
I do not believe that there is
A no left in me
If you come to me and the fire
The hunger rises between us

That being said
The timing is up to you
I have no agenda, no timetable
Come to me tomorrow
Come to me in a month
In six months
In a year

I am here
I follow guidance of Spirit
To the best of my ability

My focus is becoming more simple Every day
To love
To heal
To learn
To grow
To give all I am able
Moving with the flow
It changes and demands I change in harmony

I will only break if I become rigid
Having tasted that and caused pain
To myself and others
I leap into faith and trust
of that which brought me here

Life is short
I do not want to maybe live fully tomorrow
I only have today

What we decide is between us

Bread-crumb Blues
02-04-10

Did I know that having you in my bed
Would make me miss you so?
Don't think I really gave it much thought
As the hunger already had me in its thrall
I thought I was used to its ebb and flow
Maybe it was listening to Soon last night
Hearing more dimensions to it
Since our flesh to flesh connection

I wonder if the only easy way to be embodied
Is achieved with enlightenment
In my path though, the body is considered a blessing
Just as the Tibetans remind us that it is a precious gift
To achieve human form as spiritual growth is possible then

The Divine Lady reminds me that all acts of love and
pleasure are sacred
Belonging to her
Her rituals
Perhaps that is my answer then
The gift was in the loving

I have contemplated a lot the last couple of days
The wounds we each carry
The healing that we can give
And receive from each other
The depth and complexity we each carry
Bright and dark aspects both need to be acknowledged
Made fully conscious
And loved equally

I have to remind myself of this
For years I ran and hid from my shadow
In doing that it became the monster under the bed
Rather than just a part of me that needed to be held in
the Light
Spirit reminds me that it does not create broken
Just works in progress

in any case
The shadow of insecurity and blues and lonesomeness
Is just part of what arises in the process of loving you
Part of the shadow play
Playing peek-a-boo with me, and I respond to it:
I see you - I know you - You are part of me - you do
not rule this Heart.

There is no crisis
There is no lack of love
There is no problem

Our bond is strong and true
Like the golden filaments of light that connect me to
The Mother Earth
We are connected in Love and Light
I release my fears once again
And see they are no more substantial
Than the fluff that blows off the dandelion
In that first windy gust of Spring.

Water and Fire
11-23-09

Water and Fire am I
Supported by Earth and Air
I leap from the peak
The Air rises to embrace me
As form shifts and my wings spread
In an expanse of feathered glory and muscled strength
Swooping upon currents of air
Spirals carry me up or down
As I will
This ride is free for those of my nature

To leap the forest green
Race through paths only I see
Wait to see which of the young bucks
Shall win the fight
Come to plant their seed
The young shall come next season
Dappled coats in the sunlight
I will teach them when to be still
What scents to seek
What scents to run from
Where to rest
Where to feed
When the time comes for them
Where to mate

The greatest hunger I carry
In this tiny human form
Is the hunger to return to the Wildness
My Mother and Father
To sleep by pure mountain streams
To hear them wake me
To feel the thunder and lightning
Shake the trees around me
My heart hungers for the real life
In my bones in my blood
Ancient rhythms beg me to return

Love is not a tame being
It is fierce
It is violent
It expels all that is not itself
It demands more than I know I can give
It demands that I listen
It demands that I run
It demands that I dance

It demands that I sing its song
Alone in the wilderness
With only the stars and the moon to hear me

It laughs when I seek to make one thing its object
Too small
Too tight
Too restricted
It screams
In the song of the wind
The shriek of raptor diving for prey frozen in its tracks.

Loving you in the Sweet Time
07-13-11

I can still feel you next to me
smell your scent on my skin
feel the silver stubble on your chin
remember how still my mind was
how deep and rich my breathing
when you were doing the healing of Spirit
after we did the mutual healing of Flesh

One of the deepest joys I carry is walking a path
Where these are acknowledged as One.

I have never wanted to romance a man like I do you
I want to make your eyes light up
I want to make your smile dazzle me as it has from the
first
I want your heart to leap with joy when you see me
　　　As mine does when my eyes can devour you

I want to take long walks with you
In the sunny days on beach or woodland paths
in the fog when the mystery lays thick on the land
In the rain refreshing the night
　　　I want to lay with you on the fragrant ground
　　　where Nature welcomes us and our loving

I want to lay by you in our own small cabin
by a fireplace with blazing cedar logs
where my flesh is heated by being next to you
more than the wood that burns in the hearth fire

I want to make love all night long
fall asleep in your arms
　　　rise with the dawn wanting you again
　　　as if we had not yet begun
　　　Loving each other

I want to hear your voice in the morning
Telling me of your heart your desires
the flights of your spirit that you delight in sharing
listening as my eyes
answer you while my lips think of other things to do
than speak.

Love-light Manifesto
02-19-10

these things and that
Pine trees with their seeds showing
Nothing sexier
Fog embracing the mountain
the connection sensed between
the fire at the heart of matter
center of light in the perfect darkness

The taste of Goddess above containing all
Goddess below feeding all
shivers rise through the warmth
At the center of my being
As Love overwhelms my senses

All is Love
Atoms of Light
White Bones supporting form
This vehicle a gift
Only growing older has made me appreciate
Recognizing each day I inhabit a new body
Continuity an illusion
born anew each morning with the rising sun

Each night I journey to the world's end
Bringing back gifts
Sometimes of joy
Sometimes of sorrow
Sometimes vulnerable
Sometimes strong
Sometimes in stillness that is peace
Sometimes in stillness that is waiting
Between what is and what is next
You know
That moment

Sometimes that moment is a whole day

Love can arise like a thunderstorm
it can rise as fire inflaming
It can arise as water so fierce it carves the face of
stone
it can arise as air breathing life from you to me
it can arise as deep comfort only Earth Mother can give
It dances in motes of sunlight
It shines in the nuances in your eyes
It vibrates in the millions of voices
Whispering
Laughing
Singing
Crying out passion for life in all its glory

Though I vanish into and out of form
Life Is Everlasting
Perfect
All Embracing
Surpassing thought and thinker
Revelation in one distilled drop

of Joy

Heart-Song
03-03-10

There are voices that are stronger
Sweeter or more soulful
but this is my voice
this is my song
Straight from the heart
I can sing it for whom I will

For the Mother in her myriad forms
Earth Sea Night Sky Perfection of Space
For the God in his perfect manifestations
Horned or winged – Sphere of Light
Powerful Intelligent Penetrating

But this song I sing tonight
Is for you

I have spent time the last few days
Contemplating
Other than Reiki
What can I give
In these times of testing

Boundaries are important
There are healthy limits
To what we can do for each other
Just as the Gods themselves do not interfere
In the exercise of free will
Boundaries allow us to touch
to share
As we will

To draw back
To seek solitude and our own voice
As we will
But I can give you my song
It is free
Its melody weaves love that asks for nothing
Love that plays as the breeze plays upon your skin and hair
Love that stirs as the ocean surf crashing on the beach
Love that sits still and calm

From that calm deep center
I weave my song
as spider woman wove the first world
from the light fibers of her own body

As the Fates weave our lives into threads
Of becoming
Being
Ending
this song is light and weightless
Yet strong and warm
I weave it as a blanket to wrap around yourself
when you are quietly slipping off to the dream-time

This song is forged
from gold
Rising from the volcanic heart
Center of the planet
Center of my being
Heart fire that is molten and flowing
Liquid gold shaped
as a strong tensile barrier
To feelings of depression and loss
Grief over another's change bringing wyrd
May it help you
As it helps me
To grab hold tightly
Let go lightly

This song is melodic
as birdsong at morning light
or evensong in the time between
Dark and light
Reminding one of fearless flight
Of deep repose
Freedom from care
Perfect harmony
Its pitch is true
Is tonal octaves reflecting
the solar majors
the lunar minors
mingling and changing from one to another
As life
Never static

this song is the only gift I can give
May you use it
As you will
Some day I will sing it for you

Deep Sea Diving
08-23-11

The last week has shown me
That I have started to deep sea dive
But have not found my sea legs as of yet
Whether visuals on the acupuncture table
or at home in that state between waking and dreaming
Or receiving sudden awareness of another presence
Such as in Reiki II
or receiving strong emotional input
The input is coming faster than the skill set to navigate

This is both exhilarating and unnerving to the degree
That discretion and the map reading tools need to be developed
Perception is not merely seeing or hearing or feeling with
deeper sensory levels
But being able to interpret what the message is
My customary response of directing Reiki at everything
is calming on both ends I am sure
But not satisfying to my desire to know
Who are the players and to what degree is the impact of
the perception
requiring action

and having an inquiring mind
What does it mean?

Feel a bit like the fledgling thrown out of the nest
the wings alone do not enable flight
But knowing how to use them and what the prevailing
conditions are
how to be safe and not crash and burn

When I was younger all was blind faith and trust and openness
I survived that stage but learned there is more necessary
In order to develop skillful means.

Volcano Dancer
10-07-10

Virgin maid not by choice
At the point of sacrifice
Her dreams of passion and fiery love
Fiercer than the fear of flame
Her spirit leapt before her body burned
Free to soar above those she would never again
Call her kin

I choose the path of fire
That calls me in a sweeter siren song
Than that which enticed me before
Warmth for my bones
Warmth for my heart
Warmth to stir the memories
Of Love known many lifetimes
Still that which causes me to willingly
Dance volcano edge
Approach change fearlessly

Even in the nightmare last night
Doing the LBR
Though my voice lost its powerful chant
I spoke the last words though
Bombarded by fear
Then I told my ex
We are not living in a house haunted by such demons
Hmmm
I have the feeling there are many messages here

At least if I was dreaming a horror movie
I had enough sense to say
Baby, we are moving out now!

I will not be a victim of my own
Delusions fears or past histories
I reach for that which is free within me
It shall fly and soar on the updraft
As my brother crows show me every day
With joy and laughter

Skin Shivers
08-18-11

Held it together
Cause I had to
If the damn burst too soon before your return
The time waiting would have had me crawling up the walls
As it is making it from last night
to whenever I can hear your voice
touch you
is going to be hard enough

Last night I was wound so tight
from the commute from hell
changing the sheets on the bed
just holding the pillow against my skin
while sliding it into the pillowcase
made all my nerve endings scream

Once I was finally in bed and unsuccessfully
attempting to relax enough to sleep
I realized I could no longer hold off giving
my body the release it was starving for
I have so many moments with you I can bring to mind
There are few places on my body that I do not think
of as erogenous zones any more

Shall I tell you?
I thought about it on the drive home
your bites on my inner thighs
your slaps on my buttocks
your licking or fingers inside me
your sucking on my neck
pinching my breasts
but not too hard as you know how sensitive they are

my finger in your mouth
my hands around your cock
with just enough lubricant to make it easy to move
while holding you tightly enough
the taste of you in my mouth
the smell that is unique to you

your lips
your beard when it is just a little rough
and shines with silver bits.

How you felt when I was laying on my belly
and you were spread out on top of me
kissing my neck and such sweetness coming from you
As I have more often seen your fierce hunger
those moments of sweetness caused me to come
completely
undone.

I could go on for quite awhile
but I want to build this hunger
until we can both feed to our satisfaction
skin to skin.

The more heat that is generated between us
The deeper my love for you
I remind myself of this when the depth of my
obsession
starts to make me uneasy or insecure.

We are so much.

Songs
06-12-11

There are the songs that I sing
Anthony is a song I sing
Always melodic sometimes in the minor key
Often in the major
But the harmony of it runs through and underneath
my life
This song has its roots in other times and other lives
And it will be sung throughout this one

There is a song I sing for and with my spiritual family
This goes from the silent song of focus within
A song of stillness which weaves the concert of magic
To the full throated song I sing with full orchestra
You bring out my best song
The song I did not know I could carry
and you weave me in and out of your individual parts
Making the song deeper and richer with each round
There are always surprising new harmonies and melodies
That arise when we come together

There are sweet songs that I make up
Yesterday on the table when the needles were being
very good to me
calming and soothing and healing after the more intense
Part one
Or the songs and chants that come up in my joy
at walking the earth talking to the trees
and watching Nature cavort through all living things

Then, as in last night
There are the Songs that Sing me
Reiki Sang me the Crystal on the altar Sang me
Sang my heart open Sang all the energy I could handle
through me
blasting away obstructions like a torrent of rapidly
moving water
Brilliant and overwhelming it played me and drew out the best
this instrument was capable of

I was up much of the night before my strings lay still again

Waking up so slowly now
I am tired and very very happy.

Be Careful What You Ask For
06-17-10

Laughing
I was standing at the check printer
I was thinking about my life right now
Thinking about having asked for transformation
With all my energy about a year ago

Giving up on love in the realm of Eros
At that time
Despairing of making progress and growth
In my studies
A lot of desire pent up
In both these arenas
Resulted in those petitions to the Universe
Which are borne of blood, sweat and tears
In those moments of complete solitude

A few days after the fall Equinox
The first transformative experience
Sprung fully born out of circumstances
When I was seeking to serve with Reiki
In a new way
I met a man who I guarantee has and will continue
To change my life in unforeseen ways
Beyond anything I have ever imagined
At least not in the detail and challenge
To grow
The prime taste of it is intensity and transformation
In thought, in spirit in body and in heart.

The other is ongoing and has taken a longer struggle
To coalesce
I am approaching learning with curiosity
Joy and optimism
Granted, I am aware of the speed at which my cohorts
Rise to the occasion
But then, that is part of my challenge
To find what works for me
Put all the energy I can muster into it
Without dropping pieces that are already established
And necessary for my spiritual well being
To rejoice in the acuity of my comrades
Without comparison or regret
For the length of time it takes me to learn some lessons

Today I printed out forty three pages
Of an astrological reading on the relationship
That is a dominant influence in my life right now
I remember after watching the copies roll off the
printer at home
And catching bits and pieces of examination of my psyche
Asking myself do I really want to look at this?
This is what made me laugh at the copier
I have asked and asked and asked for the ability to change
To drop that which no longer serves me or the whole
I can run and I can hide if I choose
But that change will capture me the easy way
Or the hard way
I will get what I have bargained for and more
It has been promised.

Naked in the Rain
01-17-10

Went to bed at ten
The usual time
Only to be awakened for unknown reasons
At one am in the morning
Finally accepting I am awake
At least for now
Not sleepy
I have opened the windows a bit
To listen to the rain

Laying in my bed
Before I got up
I had an overwhelming desire
to go stand naked in the rain

Being as it is cold
and I have not yet learned the invisibility spell
I resisted the impulse
But ask myself where it sprang from

Since driving became part of the work
I do
To sustain myself in the material world
I feel both closer and further from the joys
Of the natural world

Rain and wind and fog
Become extra challenges on the roadways
Added to the main one, which unfortunately
Is other people
I was delighted to read what a friend
A new driver, had written recently
About her experience of the driving experience
As orchestrated with the classical music she plays
That is the best case scenario
One to be cultivated and enjoyed

In the morning drives, when there is the most aggression
In those compelled to travel to their destination as fast
as possible
I am still often captured by the beauty of the new day
dawning
Especially as I go through the micro climates from the
East Bay
To North Bay
Approaching the area close to Mount Tamalpais
Which calls me to come visit it some day

So there is the contrast between humans
in their dangerous little tin cans
Rushing their lives away
and the Stillness manifesting
In the perfection of Nature
Its cycles of day and night
The seasons
Its time of rest
Its time of bearing fruit

In dancing naked in the rain
I wanted to taste that Perfection
Let my body delight in the bond with Life

I Bend, Love, I Will Not Break
05-30-10

Finishing this morning's yoga practice
The first taste of this poem came to me
Reflecting on my mother's words yesterday
As she reminded me of the strength in my ancestors
She knows she has reserves to draw upon
They are in her very bones

As my body is supple and stronger now
Than in my youth
So is my spirit and my heart and my will
I aim my arrows at the target chosen
Release the string and they fly
Letting go in that instant
As I have done my job
The outcome rests in Being

My heart learns anew each day
what it means to love
Sifting through the chaff
of selfish desires
expectations
wants
dreams of the future
To find its natural resting place once again
To just be Love in this instant
There is only now
In this moment Love rules
and my kingdom is perfect

My spirit seeks knowledge
Wisdom
Experience
Kinship
Community
Service
Joy

as the Holy fool
I leap off the precipice
Knowing if the arms of the Angels
Do not receive me
then my wings shall sprout forth
To carry me on the winds of Heaven
Lightly to land once again on my Mother Earth
Kissing her with Gratitude

A Pocketful of Maybes
04-09-10

Brother of my soul
I pray you are stronger than me
More constant
Sometimes it gets so hard
To just trust that Spirit
Which holds my birth and death
And all in between in its hand
Holds my heart through the love I bear you
As well

I know that Love makes no demands
Gives of itself freely
But there are certainly times when I feel
So very very human
Just a woman who wants her man
No matter what right I have to want you
What is exists in the beating of my heart
Desire that courses through my blood
If I had it to do all over again
Other than the bits of my cruelty that surfaced
I would not change a thing

Why do poets and writers write?
Why do artists and musicians hone their craft?
If I did not have this page to pour my true heart upon
There would be no outlet

If I did not have your ear
Non judgmental and kind as you have always been
I would not love you as much
Or feel as free to express everything I feel

It is safe to do so now
Between us we immolated the dark negative bits that hurting me
Arose to hurt you

I keep my longing in a bag of silk
Hanging in my window the Spring breezes
Tease it with the scent of flowers
If it gets too heavy the bag will break
Scattering bits of desire upon the floor

The last bunch of white stargazer lilies were locally grown
They are huge and fragrant
Though my offerings to the ancestors and purifications
have been sporadic
The peace and strength still exists; I never let the
offering bowl go empty
Until the next time I catch that moment to do the work
Before I am too tired and retire

Last night just before sleeping
I put up the Lemurian crystal and my healing wand
They accidentally struck each other and made a spark of
visible light

There was no damage to either

Christine Berger

A Perfect Golden Love of a Day
08-05-10

Did I have to be squeezed through the crucible
of my own flaming slag this past weekend to get to this
Day of grace
Day of love
Day of giving and receiving in simplicity

Goddess knows that without these rest periods
I would not have the strength to do more
than crawl across the floor

Instead as GIFU indicated this morning
This was a Gift from whatever Divine forces
Keep watch as those of us form bound
Do our best to unite the energies of heaven and earth
within and without

Tonight I danced as offering
I offered a poem as reading in the 12 step room
I took chances reaching out
I once again affirmed that my life
Is to serve that which is unknowable
Unnameable
But which expresses and speaks to me in the voice
of Love that is so immense
I am rocked in it like a baby at its
Mother's breast

So I ride these currents
That carry me
With all the attention I can muster
Gathering information as I listen
In five minutes at work this morning when
Writing to my dear love
Every song was a communication
with the code to right action
Instructions on how to love
when to surrender
when to trust
when to simply rejoice
That I am part of this Life
This Love
This dance of Light and Dark
Entwined as the oldest of lovers
Soul-mated

Burn, Baby, Burn
12-03-09

I burn
Deep inside the core is where this fire lives
Like the hunger that cannot be assuaged
I am learning to live with it
To tend it
For all intensive purposes
I carry it alone
Fanning the flames until I can bear no more
I take that heat and send it through my body
Healing
Gathering the old pains and hurts and letting them
Be tinder

I am learning to live within these depths
Alone
The earth will comfort me when I go to Her
As will her son, her lover
The Horned God
I will not depend on any other resolution
The present is empty
The future not guaranteed
And shadowed by necessity

Last night I laughed after I wrote the last poem
Looking at one of my several
Favorite astrological forecasts for the week
I was told I would need to work on reconciling
opposites
You think?
Nothing else will end this torment
I cannot depend on anything outside myself as solution
I will swim these deep waters
Until the water is like a second skin to me
Waters of birth
Waters of death
Waters of transformation

I have given up on any resolution
Now I just have to give up thinking of this situation
Of fire and water and hunger and need
As a problem
Find a way to revel in it
Turn the pain of it to joy
With or without you here

Aftermath of 0=0
08-09-09

He comes
He comes in spirit within
He comes in ritual calling
He comes in secret hours of the night
He comes in the brightness of perfect dawn
He comes in the connection of love between us
He comes in the silence when all thought is banished
And the space is prepared

Soon we will prepare the ground
It will be intensely focused
It will be willed by all who play
It will be received by each
It will be shared by all
It will benefit all

I am changing inside out
It is my intent bearing fruit
In spite of myself
It is my heart firing on all cylinders
Burning off the dross
It is the reason I am here now
As we have chosen
It is the reason we are all here now

I am changing with each breath
I am breathing through each change
I am embracing the elements
I am embracing the earth
I am embracing all that shares life with me
I am dancing with joy
I am singing with the stars in a velvet black night
I am vibrating
I am vibrating
I am vibrating

I am alive
It is the heart of the matter
It is the heart that matters
It is the change that arises
In a Universe of perfect stillness
In a Universe of still perfection

Building a bridge with broken cinder blocks
10-17-09

These are the things that happen to me
I understand why I get confused

Coming out of the bank yesterday
At about 05:00 pm
I suddenly became wet and thought of you
I have no frame of reference
Questioning my sanity is only part
Of the reason I asked for birth information
I could use a road map in the understanding
What we bring to the table in context to each other.

There is the potential for something that sure
Feels good here

This morning I was finishing up my yoga
Laying on the floor in a meditative state
Suddenly I had a thought of you and
That electricity shot up my spine again
(Hello Amp)

There is magic here
But without a grounding in reality
*(This means touching base with you)
Periodically
I have no idea if it is delusion
Reality on another level
Or simply potential

I know we connect
I know we both have issues
We have to work out
Though you know more
About what mine are than vice versa
This is really OK

As long as I know

Are we on the same page?
Or are we even reading the same book?

Smile, whatever happens
I love you
Brother of my soul....

Scouring it until it Shines
07-09-10

Sometimes the reward for scraping out the bits
Hard to look at
and giving them the full attention they deserve
Comes fast
A moment of peace
Maybe a moment of touching the innocence
That is a Heart thing
A Spirit thing
A timeless essence that is not jaded
or saddened by the struggles of one lifetime's years

Would I
I wonder
want this longing to stop
Though it has been torturous this week
Since I know that it is born from the depth of the
connection
we have
Part of me gets very insecure
when I feel incomplete without you

Didn't I spend years and years to drum into my head
That this is a sin against self
To think I need another person to complete me
I can label that thought as deluded
Yet each year of life tells me nothing is more important
Than Love
There is something uniquely powerful and compelling
about
Us

I knew a long time ago that I was not cut out to be a
full time hermit
This lifetime
My seclusion is more due to being an energy empath
Needing quiet time to recharge and find my boundaries
Reinforcing them as needed

I assume that you do not need me
Yet I should know by now that assumptions will be
the death of me
And it really is none of my business what you do or feel
Other than what you show me when we are together

It has just been a difficult week
Working at the hardest pace to make the green
Our phone time which usually acts as a safety valve
Relieving some of the pressure
Backfired and just made me want to see you more than before

Beyond all that there is that soul dissatisfaction
That we live in
Right before major shifts occur
Collectively we are on the brink
Individually we have to each carry our own weight
With enough graciousness and courage
That we are able to lend a hand to anyone who
may need it

Please know as I comb through these tangled
skeins woven within
As my current assignment

For you my darling
I am blowing kisses.

Traveling Down the Line
04-02-10

I do my best to just let it go
Knowing your world is focused on one person
As it should be
As it has to be
But I feel your pain
Remember as kids when we would play with strings and cans
Maybe you were too young
The vibration would travel down the string
A primitive form of telephone

My days have peaks of emotional pain
I accept that I am picking up on you
My thoughts are full of you much of the time, unbidden
Sometimes it hurts so bad I just cry
at some stupid thing on TV
or a movie
Knowing that is a chance to release

(Do not get me wrong, I never regret the bond that
connects us)

The only time it will stop for a bit
Is when I send Reiki
Especially at night
You are probably asleep but it flows to you anyhow
Strong and sure
I get a respite then before sleep

I don't call you or text you
I don't want to impinge on your privacy
On your boundaries
there are things we do for those we are closest to
that are sacred
They are precious moments
that mark our souls
our spirits
For lifetimes

It is important that those times have
All of our attention
All of our love
All of our essence
Given to them

When you have time and space
When your spirit moves you to do so
Contact me

It would give me a measure of peace
To hear from you
In a more direct way
Than these waves of emotion
Traveling down the line

After Kundalini
05-09-10

It was my first full class
Beginner's online
Challenging yet fun
New fresh and interesting
When I finally lay down for savasana
I started to cry
Grief poured from me
Through me
Without an object
Without an attachment

Simply the experience of grief

Somehow this made sense
To experience the emotion
To fully be within it
Without attaching anything else to it
Not why am I feeling this
No resistance to the feeling
Simply to be in that flavor

So Joy
Would be equal to Love
as sister to Sorrow
As brother to
Anger
As daughter to
Anguish
No attachment
No difference
Passing through as the stages
of caterpillar to butterfly
seed to plant
dawn to dusk

It is time to go get breakfast now.

Searching for the Phoenix
09-19-11

*If I honor my joy and delight
my heat and my flesh and my love
Then why would I disregard my despair
my sorrow my loss?*

*All are fuel for the bonfire
Upon which I burn to ash
In order for new worlds to be born*

*Always seeking stability
I forget the play of the ever changing
the anchor not circumstantial
but that fiery brightness that consumes
the old vision
While striking the match to fire the one arising*

*Freedom is not some rudderless ship
that never takes off because it goes willy nilly
chasing after this desire and then that
Freedom is honed of the will and sharp as steel
it demands precision and intelligence
as well as the surrender to perfect timing
in which to act*

or to withhold from action

*The wisest bits of me are the child
and the body
those bits that are completely unconcerned with
Being wise
Since that usually just ends up as being
a smart ass*

*Free to play, the self imposed restrictions fall away
and the one that was falling apart
Falls true straight to the center
Into the loving coils of the rising serpent.*

About Concrescent Letters

Concrescent Letters is dedicated to publishing unique works of Poetry and Prose. It takes advantage of the recent revolution in publishing technology and economics to bring forth works that, previously, might only have been circulated privately.

Now, we are growing the future together.

Colophon

This book is made of Mistral and Dakota, using Adobe InDesign. The cover was designed, the body was set by Sam Webster. Cover art of (untitled) tree drawing by Karen W. Moy.

Visit our website at
www.Concrescent.net